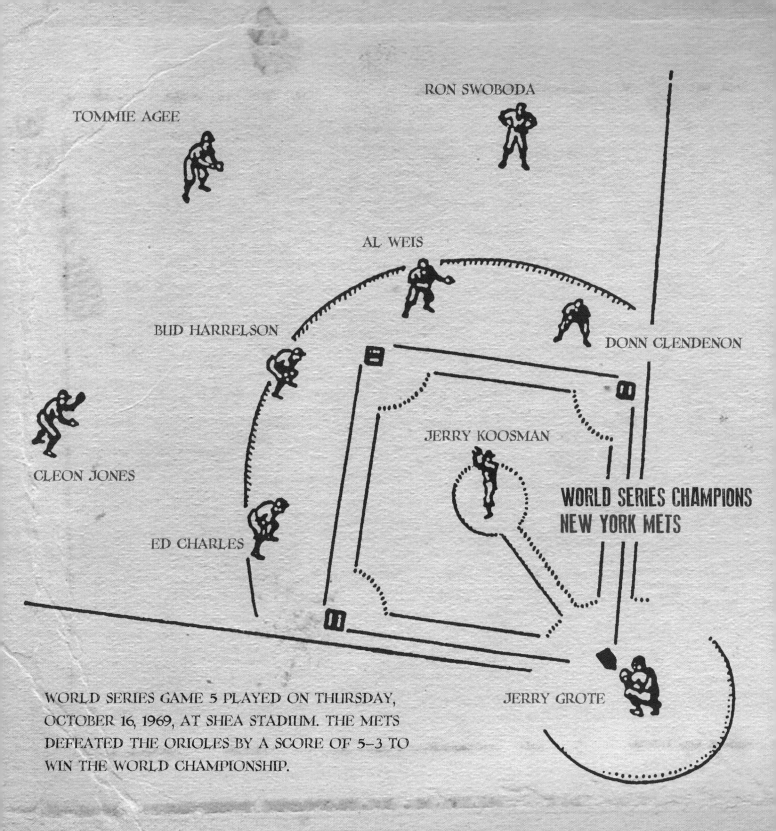

TOMMIE AGEE

RON SWOBODA

AL WEIS

BUD HARRELSON

DONN CLENDENON

CLEON JONES

JERRY KOOSMAN

WORLD SERIES CHAMPIONS
NEW YORK METS

ED CHARLES

JERRY GROTE

WORLD SERIES GAME 5 PLAYED ON THURSDAY,
OCTOBER 16, 1969, AT SHEA STADIUM. THE METS
DEFEATED THE ORIOLES BY A SCORE OF 5–3 TO
WIN THE WORLD CHAMPIONSHIP.

WORLD SERIES CHAMPIONS

NEW YORK METS

SARA GILBERT

CREATIVE EDUCATION

Published by Creative Education
P.O. Box 227, Mankato, Minnesota 56002
Creative Education is an imprint of The Creative Company
www.thecreativecompany.us

Design and production by Blue Design (www.bluedes.com)
Art direction by Rita Marshall
Printed in the United States of America

Photographs by Getty Images (Al Bello, Paul Bereswill, Bruce
Bennett Studio, Andrew D. Bernstein, Linda Cataffo/NY News
Archive, Ed Clarity/NY Daily News Archive, C. Taylor Crothers,
Stephen Dunn, Don Emmert/AFP, G Flume, Focus on Sport, Doug
Kanter/AFP, Lass, David Leeds/Allsport, Jim McIsaac, National
Baseball Hall of Fame Library/MLB Photos, Rich Pilling/MLB
Photos, Louis Requena/MLB Photos, Rogers Photo Archive, Ezra
Shaw, Keith Torrie/NY Daily News Archive, Chris Trotman, Ron
Vesely/MLB Photos, Michael Zagaris/MLB Photos)

Library of Congress Cataloging-in-Publication Data
Gilbert, Sara.
New York Mets / Sara Gilbert.
p. cm. — (World series champions)
Includes bibliographical references and index.
Summary: A simple introduction to the New York Mets major
league baseball team, including its start in 1962, its World Series
triumphs, and its stars throughout the years.
ISBN 978-1-60818-268-8
1. New York Mets (Baseball team)—History—Juvenile literature. I.
Title.
GV875.N45G55 2013
796.357'64097471—dc23 [B]   2012004262

First edition
9 8 7 6 5 4 3 2 1

Cover: Third baseman David Wright
Page 2: Second baseman Daniel Murphy
Page 3: Pitcher Billy Wagner
Right: The Mets in the 1973 World Series

SS

REY ORDOÑEZ

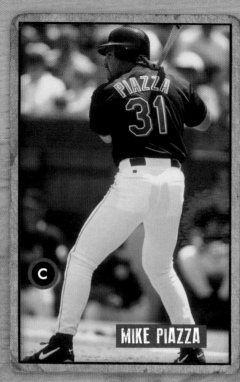

C

MIKE PIAZZA

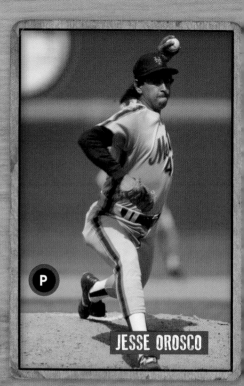

P

JESSE OROSCO

P

TOM SEAVER

CF

MOOKIE WILSON

1B

ED KRANEPOOL

TABLE OF CONTENTS

NEW YORK AND CITI FIELD

New York City is the biggest city in America. More than 8 million people live there. Many New Yorkers like to go to a ballpark called Citi Field in the summer. A baseball team called the Mets plays there.

9

RIVALS AND COLORS

The Mets are 1 of 30 teams in Major League Baseball. All the teams try to win the World Series and become world champions. The Mets' team colors are blue, orange, and white. The Philadelphia Phillies are the Mets' biggest RIVALS.

PITCHER JERRY KOOSMAN

RIGHT FIELDER DARRYL STRAWBERRY

METS HISTORY

The Mets played their first season in 1962. That year, the Mets lost 120 games. That was a new major-league RECORD. But New York fans loved their new team anyway.

In 1969, pitcher Tom Seaver helped the UNDERDOG Mets have their best season yet. He led them to the PLAYOFFS for the first time. Then he helped them win the

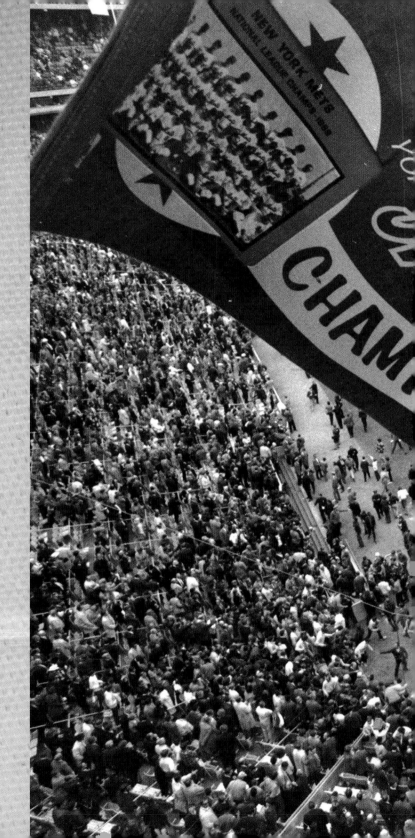

1969 WORLD SERIES

GOOD AFTERNOON
AND
THANK YOU FOR COMING
PLEASE ARRIVE HOME
SAFELY

NO THROWING
OF OBJECTS

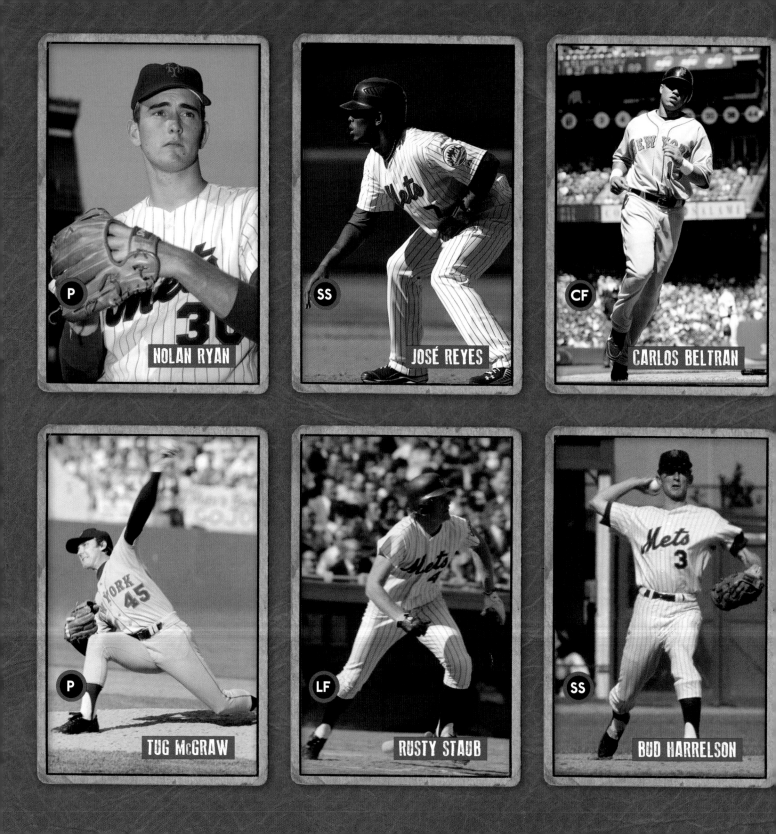

NOLAN RYAN

JOSÉ REYES

CARLOS BELTRAN

TUG McGRAW

RUSTY STAUB

BUD HARRELSON

World Series! People called them the "Miracle Mets."

The Mets returned to the World Series in 1973. But this time they lost. They went back again in 1986. First baseman Keith Hernandez helped them beat the Boston Red Sox to capture another championship!

KEITH HERNANDEZ

In 2000, slugging catcher Mike Piazza and the Mets played the New York Yankees in the World Series. The Mets lost to their **CROSSTOWN** rivals. They have not been back to the World Series since then.

MIKE PIAZZA

METS STARS

The Mets' first manager was Casey Stengel. He knew a lot about baseball. Pitcher Jerry Koosman started striking out batters with his great **CURVEBALL** in 1967. He won 140 games for the Mets.

Pitcher Dwight Gooden joined the Mets in 1984. His blazing

fastballs helped the Mets win a lot of games. Slugger Edgardo Alfonzo was another star in New York. He was a powerful hitter and a good third baseman.

In 2008, star pitcher Johan Santana joined the Mets. He struck out many batters and won 16 games in his first season in New York. He gave New York fans hope that their beloved Mets would return to the World Series soon!

EDGARDO ALFONZO

PITCHER MIKE PELFREY

HOW THE METS GOT THEIR NAME

The name "Mets" is short for "Metropolitans." That name fit the team because it was located in a metropolis, or a huge city. Another baseball team that had played in New York a long time ago was also called the Metropolitans.

ABOUT THE METS

First season: 1962

League/division: National League, East Division

World Series championships:

1969   *4 games to 1 versus Baltimore Orioles*

1986   *4 games to 3 versus Boston Red Sox*

Mets Web site for kids:

http://mlb.mlb.com/nym/fan_forum/kids_index.jsp

Club MLB:

http://web.clubmlb.com/index.html

GLOSSARY

CROSSTOWN — describing something on the other side of town

CURVEBALL — a pitch that curves away from home plate as it gets close to the batter

PLAYOFFS — all the games (including the World Series) after the regular season that are played to decide who the champion will be

RECORD — something that is the best or most ever

RIVALS — teams that play extra hard against each other

UNDERDOG — a person or team that is not expected to win

INDEX